# DESTINY CROSSROADS

**TRUSTING THE SOVEREIGNTY OF GOD IN CHALLENGING TIMES**

GAYLEAN MAYNARD

Copyright © 2025 Gaylean Sharon Maynard

ALL RIGHTS RESERVED. NO part of this book may be reproduced or transmitted in any form by any means, electronic or mechanical, including photocopying and recording, or by any information storage and retrieval system, except as may be expressly permitted in writing from the author.

ISBN: 978-1-966968-13-9

Published by:

www.owlpublishers.com

360 S Market St, San Jose, CA 95113,

United States.

Printed in the United States of America

TRUSTING THE SOVEREIGNTY OF GOD IN

CHALLENGING TIMES

## DEDICATION

To my grandson, Brayden Walker, may your desires and aspirations be expanded in your generation? I pray that Jesus Christ would be your foundation, and you would experience Father God in unprecedented ways, and because of your relentless dedication to follow Christ, countless individuals would come to know Jesus as Lord and Savior.

# APPRECIATION

Dr. Kayla Bullard, you were the answer to my prayers. Thank you for every second, minute, and hour you spent assisting me to produce this manuscript.

# FOREWORD

By: Rev. Lavette McFall BSc., MCS., J.P.

**"Destiny Crossroads"** is a must read. It is a riveting, emotionally moving testimony designed to shoot missiles that will pierce the debilitating hurts of your past while healing your brokenness as it ushers you towards your Divine appointment with destiny.
Apostle Gaylean Maynard has penned a life transforming work that not only allows one to see behind the smiles, the true story of this courageous, purpose driven author, but it contains the antidote for destiny paralysis created from her personal life of pain, doubt, fear, insecurity, rejection and unforgiveness.
This timely work is spiritually liberating for those who may be stuck at a destiny crossroad and it has the capability to transport its readers via faith to embrace the unknown.
This authentic, transparent author not only attempts to help you through her vivid life stories, but she does not leave you there; she pulls you towards the Eternal, Sovereign, All-Powerful God, her God, who brought her through, and if you journey through these enlightening pages with her and dare to believe, He has the power to bring you out too.
The core of her message unveils this truth: when your destiny crossroads are orchestrated by God, what naturally may be life defining is providentially designed by God to shift you in alignment with his established good plan for your life.
Finally, this story testifies not only of the significance of faith when encountering a destiny crossroad, but it is a catalyst to answered prayers, and a force to give you the tools to do what you have never done before.
I can assure you that at the end of this read, you will say **YES** to the voice of your destiny. Now, with all that said, I personally put my stamp of approval on this work, and if I had to choose a destiny crossroads empowering book, this author would get my vote.

# Table of Content

Introduction ................................................................. 1

Chapter 1: Leaving the Past Behind ........................... 5

Chapter 2: Change & Challenges ............................. 12

Chapter 3: Courage & Faith ..................................... 20

Chapter 4: When Destiny Calls ................................ 28

Chapter 5: Moving Forward In Faith ....................... 33

Chapter 6: Joy and Newness .................................... 37

Chapter 7: Walking In Favor ................................... 40

Chapter 8: The Outcome ......................................... 46

Chapter 9: Good News ............................................ 50

What does the bible say? .......................................... 55

About The Author .................................................. 57

About The Book ..................................................... 59

# INTRODUCTION

Life's journey takes us through many different pathways. Sometimes, we experience trauma, pain, death, disaster, roadblocks, disappointments, and setbacks. "Destiny Crossroads" are unscheduled moments or intersections in life. These unscripted and unforeseen issues cause us to make life-altering decisions that challenge us in unsurmountable ways, thus often significantly changing our future.

According to Webster's New Pocket dictionary, the word 'destiny' means one's fate, position, or outcome in life. A *"Destiny Crossroad"* can be viewed as an encounter causing an individual to make a series of decisions that can alter a person's emotional, physical, or spiritual growth. This decision can have either a negative or positive impact and can result in either bondage or freedom. These *"Destiny Crossroad"* occasions are the uncertain, crucial, and defining periods experienced in one's life.

Dear reader, even though life's challenges may come our way, there is hope in God—our Father, who is always leading and directing our pathway. If you are reading this book and don't have a relationship with God, it means that you have not accepted Jesus Christ as your Lord and personal Savior. In that case, I pray that my story will transform your life. Furthermore, as you reflect on your own life, I want you to envision you're past and current *"Destiny Crossroad"* experiences. Reflect on how they have shaped your life. Let me assure you that we must look to God for directions when we find ourselves at the intersection with destiny. Only when we acknowledge God can we have confidence and assurance that the outcome of what we are facing will work out for our good, ACCORDING TO THE WORD OF GOD!

In my own life, I have experienced many situations, some positive and some negative. I will share several personal life-changing moments that significantly transformed my life. What saw me through each challenge was my unwavering faith in God. I trusted the Lord's strategic timing, read the Bible, prayed, and fasted. That was the catalyst that pushed me through each season.

To parallel my story, I will draw from the book of Ruth in the Bible. Ruth made numerous life-altering decisions. She was not your average woman. She was married to a man who was despised by her countrymen. She was barren and destitute. Since Ruth's husband, father-in-law, and brother-in-law had died, she had to choose where she would live for the remainder of her life.

Along with her sister-in-law, Orpah Ruth had to make a real-time decision about whether to leave Moab and go to Bethlehem in Judah with their Jewish mother-in-law. In Ruth 1:14, *"Orpah and Ruth lifted their voices and wept; and Orpah kissed her mother-in-law, goodbye, but Ruth held onto her."* Ruth's decision to cling or hold on to Naomi was a life-altering decision that would forever change her life. Ruth's bold, unorthodox decision to travel to a foreign land impacted her and Naomi's lives, thus altering the course of Jewish history.

Let me prophetically declare, dear reader, that God has a plan for your life. As you read my story, see it as your own life. Ask the God of the universe to guide you and reveal His plans for your life. Dear reader, your destiny is not defined by your painful past, your current, or future experiences. The Word of God in Jeremiah 29:11-13 says, *"For I know the plans and thought that I have for you, says the Lord, plans for peace and well-being and not for disaster, to give you a future and a hope. Then you will call on me, and you will come and pray to me, and I will hear, and I will listen to you. Then you will seek me and find me when you search for me with all your heart."* Know that God and not you are responsible for your destiny.

As you read with hope and expectation,

Open your mind and ask the Lord to speak to you,
because you will be challenged.
Peruse each page slowly, and as you ponder each crucial moment in <u>my life</u>, take a pen pad, and chronicle how my encounters are similar to your own experiences.

# DESTINY CROSSROADS/TRUSTING THE SOVEREIGNTY OF GOD IN CHALLENGING TIMES

# DESTINY CROSSROADS/TRUSTING THE SOVEREIGNTY OF GOD IN CHALLENGING TIMES

# CHAPTER 1: LEAVING THE PAST BEHIND

I loved my profession, but most of all, serving the people of the Bahamas. I resigned in August 2002 after working for 20 years with a government agency. One morning, as I was processing some paperwork at my desk, I heard a still small voice, "Gaylean, if you do not leave this career, you will miss me." Instantly, peace flowed throughout my inner being, overwhelming me from my head to my toes. Every strain of hair on my head stood at attention as I recognized that it was the voice of the Holy Spirit.

Flooded with peace and confidence, I knew I had to resign, so I spoke with a friend who helped me write my resignation letter. My then-boss was shocked when I presented him with this letter since it was so abrupt and unexpected. Nevertheless, he wished me well in my future endeavors, as he was confident that I would succeed wherever I went. I immediately began clearing my office space. This was not an easy task as I was resigning from a 20-year career that I dearly loved, leaving a community and an island I called home.

Having resigned from my job, I decided that a change of pace was the answer, and as a result, I decided to move to the city of Nassau, the capital city of the Bahamas. Nassau is located on the island of New Providence, the busiest Bahamian island in the archipelago. The opportunity to reinvent me was much more likely and imaginable. Knowing of the potential options in Nassau gave me a sense of peace, excitement, and anticipation about starting a new life there. However, uncertainty loomed in the distance. Confidently, I moved forward in faith, responding to the Holy Spirit's still small voice and my belief in the Bible. I found solace in one of my favorite scriptures, Proverbs 3:5-6:

Trust in the Lord with all your heart and lean not on your understanding,

In all your ways, submit to him, and he will make your paths straight.

Resigning my occupation meant giving up my financial security and status in life. Therefore, I expected my family in Nassau, New Providence, to question me about how I would support myself and where I would live. Despite the peace, I felt, indubitably stamped at the forefront of my mind were the potential challenges I would have to face. Issues of uncertainty, namely family relational matters, that I knew would be looming. I was determined to obey God's voice. I had a "Destiny Crossroad" experience as I was methodically and thoughtfully packing. The decision to obey God, resign from my job, and relocate to another island would certainly change my life.

While packing, I reflected on Ruth's life, pondering the resemblances between our lives. Ruth was a Moabite from the lineage of Lot. The Moabites were an accursed race resulting from the incestuous sexual relationship between Lot and his daughter after a drunken episode. The son who was born to the oldest daughter was named Moab. Historically, the Moabites worshipped many gods. Chemosh was the chief god they celebrated and revered as the god of fertility and honored as the protector of Moab. Ruth, who grew up serving as a harlot priestess, performed lustful orgies with the fertility goddess in the temple. Moab's people also engaged in human sacrifice. In I Kings, the king of Moab offered his son as a burnt sacrifice to invoke help from Chemosh when the people of Moab were at war with Israel.

Israel's prophets, Amos, Isaiah, Jeremiah, and Ezekiel, all prophesied Moab's destruction because of their lustful, sinful, and diabolical acts. Like me, Ruth was religious and served numerous gods, but I serve only one, the sovereign Creator of the universe. He is one God known as God the Father, Jesus Christ, and the Holy Spirit, one God with many names and functions.

The relationship between Moabites and Israel was tumultuous because they were relatives also friends and foes. The Bible records many events about their interconnections. In Numbers 25:1-2, after Israel's children left Egypt, Moab's women led the men of Israel into sexual sin against God. Furthermore, in Deuteronomy 23:3, the people of Israel were forbidden to admit the Moabites into the temple of the Lord. Even though they shared kinship and history, Moab and Israel's conflict led to competition and strife between them. The ongoing clash between Moab and Israel resulted in a love-hate interrelationship that clouded and laced their contextual historical story. When Ruth met her husband, Mahlon, she had to make a life-altering choice to marry him. Marrying Mahlon meant that they would experience much criticism and rejection.

# DESTINY CROSSROADS/TRUSTING THE SOVEREIGNTY OF GOD IN CHALLENGING TIMES

Naomi and her husband, Elimelech, and their two sons, Mahlon and Chilion, moved to Moab because of Bethlehem's famine. Naomi's sons married women who gave up their religion, beliefs, and traditions to embrace their spouses' practices and spiritual principles. Eastern marriage during that time required women to take on the ethnic culture of their spouses. The Bible does not record the specifics of Ruth's life with her husband; therefore, we must use our imagination. I imagine that life was not easy for Ruth and her husband, Mahlon.

Naomi's family had made a life-altering choice when they migrated from Judea to the land of Moab. Ruth's sacrifice was significant as she had to give up her way of life. Perhaps she had lost family and friends when she decided to marry a Jewish man. Ruth's first Destiny encounter was manifested when she chose to become one with her husband.

Similarly, in my first book, "Behind the Smiles," I tell the story of how I suffered the pain of emotional and physical abuse for ten (10) years at the hands of my ex-husband. The decision to run for my life changed my entire future. If I had not moved when I did, there was a real possibility that I would have eventually died at the hands of my ex-husband. The decision I made to leave has caused me to experience much. Just like Ruth, I had to leave my home and talk about my experiences that brought exposure to domestic violence in a small, close-knit community.

However, many of my friends who hid their pain bitterly resented me for speaking so explicitly about domestic violence. Being shunned by the people whom I had called friends and family was emotionally exhausting; by breaking the secret code of silence, I was made to suffer. The ostracizing intensified, and along with it, there was the feeling of rejection and hopelessness. Ruth and I understood what it meant to stand alone and make a life-altering decision. When Ruth decided to marry Mahlon, she wanted a loving marriage and a new way of life. On the other hand, when I went public about domestic violence, I wanted out of an abusive marriage because I deserved more and wanted a spouse who loved and valued me.

Naomi and her daughters-in-law, Ruth and Oprah, became widows through unknown circumstances. Rather than remain in Moab without any support or provisions, Naomi decided to return home to Judea because she had heard that her country's famine was over. When Ruth's husband, father-in-law, and brother-in-law died, she was hopeless as she did not have a protector. I could vividly envision Naomi's uncertainty about returning home as a widower with the added responsibility of her daughter-in-law, Ruth. Depressed and discouraged, Naomi told Ruth and Oprah to remain in Moab because she could not promise them a better way of life. Consumed with brokenness and bitterness, Naomi begged them not to follow her because she had nothing to offer them.

Oprah retreated, but Ruth was resolute in that she was going with her mother-in-law, for she declared in Ruth I: 16-17, "Where you go, I will go, where you stay, I will stay, your people will be my people and your God, my God. Where you die, I will die, and there I will be buried. May the Lord deal with me, be it ever so severely, if even death separates you and me." Ruth's relentless decision to follow Naomi yet again put her at a place of "Destiny Crossroad."

Just like me, Ruth was clueless about her future. She had no idea what to expect. However, she loved and trusted her mother-in-law and, as a result, decided to leave Moab and relocate to Bethlehem. Ruth was willing to leave the past behind and embrace new ethnic and cultural differences. Ruth freely dedicated her future to her mother-in-law and resolved that her former heathen ways were no longer an option. Following Naomi offered her freedom and exposure to new possibilities.

Exhaling, I packed, just like Ruth; I was thinking about the uncertainties surrounding the decision I had made. I was clueless about my future. Waves of emotions washed over me, but I was convinced that I had made the right decision. My faith in God propelled me forward. Giving up a 20-year career, security, and my home's comfort to move to a new city was an enormous feat. I was driven by a quiet peace that filled my soul even though to others,, what I was doing was senseless. To me, it was the perfect resolution.

Therefore, I moved quickly because the sinister enemies of doubt and unbelief were closely hovering over me to steal my peace and assurance in God. I convincingly put my future into the hands of an unseen God as I responded to His directives, although not knowing the outcome. Some would say that the decision that both Ruth and I made was impulsive, but I chose to say we were pacesetters who took a quantum leap of faith that forever changed our lives.

Ruth, who had to contend with the reality of being an outsider in Judea, nevertheless, moved in faith and trust and followed her mother-in-law. Undoubtedly, she wondered what it would be like to live in a country that was different from Moab. I am sure she pondered what it would be like to be an outsider without her husband's protection to keep her safe from dwelling among strangers. Maybe Ruth was hopeful that she would find happiness in this new place. I am sure Ruth was anxious and pondered whether she would be accepted as a Moabite since her nation, the Israelites, was often in conflict.

Ruth, like me, had more questions than answers about her future. Her decision to follow Naomi was an indication of her willingness to let go of her uncertainties and sacrifice herself to help her mother-in-law. Ruth's unselfish choice of following Naomi resulted in her marriage to a wealthy kinsman-redeemer, Boaz, the grandfather of King David, and so Ruth became an ancestor of the greater David, Jesus Christ.

## My Prophetic release over your life!

Lord Jesus, I speak peace to the person reading this book right now, especially if they are experiencing a difficult time now, which would require them to make life-altering decision(s).

Friend(s), pause and consider asking the Lord Jesus Christ to help you in your moment of crisis.

He wants to help you, that is why He died on the cross of Calvary,

Jesus died, and the suffering He experienced was for you and me. He wants to help you with your pains and heartaches.

In simple childlike faith, open your mouth and heart and ask the Lord Jesus Christ to come into your life and be the Lord of your present and future.

**Dear Reader, DON'T** feel pressured to repeat

The following prayer, you can always come back to this page anytime you WANT! However, if you are feeling uncertain about your future, I would encourage you to re-read chapter one before moving to chapter two

## Your prayer!

Jesus Christ, I _____ (say your name)
Surrender my will to you, Jesus.

I give you all my pains, heartaches, cares, and concerns especially the things that I cannot control.
Jesus, I ask that your divine purpose and plan for my life be revealed in Jesus's name.

I confess that I have tried doing things my way, and I have made a mess of my life.

Jesus, I confess that I want to follow you and
I want you to direct my life in the path you have planned,
before I was conceived in my mother's womb.

........................

## My Prophetic release over your life!

Friend, if you have prayed that simple prayer, you have just engaged in a spiritual relationship (covenant) with God, and through faith He has become your Lord and personal Savior.

You may not feel anything, and you may be wondering if your confession was legitimate.

Let me assure you that it was. Your new relationship with God is not predicated on feelings but instead on Faith and Trust.

The words you spoke were faith-filled words spoken to a Holy God, and He acknowledged every Word you spoke in faith.

As you seek out a faith-filled church (a group of like-minded believers),
spend time reading the Word of God and praying/talking to Jesus
You will begin to experience spiritual growth,

your walk with the Father will deepen, and you will learn to hear His voice when He speaks.

The time will come when you have your own Ruth experiences and rewards!

........................

**My prayer for you!**

Lord Jesus, I pray that your wisdom and Love will comfort my friend.

Heavenly Father, let your presence overshadow my friend right now and consume him or her with your Love. Give _____ (say your name) faith now!

Lord Jesus, to trust you with his/her future.

Direct _____ (say your name) to a faith-based church so he/she can be taught how to serve you and grow in Love and grace. Reader, I believe that because you committed today to follow Christ that your future will be better than your past and present.

And just like Ruth and myself, you will have a glorious encounter with Jesus Christ.

# CHAPTER 2: CHANGE & CHALLENGES

What I failed to mention was that I was making a solo move. My girls had already relocated, and as a result, my work had become my life. Even though I wanted to leave the island for three years, I could not find a way to do so. I applied numerous times for a transfer to another location, but my transfer was rejected each time. However, despite each rejection, I continued to dedicate myself to the job. My coworkers became an extension of my family, while my clients became my life. I was attached to them; therefore, I looked forward to serving them daily and addressing their concerns. Helping with their needs caused me temporally to forget what I was dealing with at home. Departing the community made my leaving very traumatic, and I had to push through my anxiety and fear to embrace new beginnings. Making a transition is never easy, especially when one must say goodbye to the person whom one loves.

The day I departed was very emotional and tear-filled; as the plane took off, I cried uncontrollably. Even though I had peace in my soul, my heart was torn because of leaving my accustomed life behind. I was also anxious about how I would engage with and respond to my estranged family, who were waiting for me in New Providence. However, just like Ruth, who was determined to leave Moab. I had made a definitive decision to relocate, and there was no turning back. Settling in Nassau presented many challenges. The most significant adjustment I had to make was finding living accommodations as I was an independent individual accustomed to living only with my daughters, making the mental and emotional adjustment to living with new people uncomfortable and uncertain.

My mother lived alone and needed assistance; I also needed somewhere to live. For me, relocating to my mother's house was another "destiny crossroad." Deciding to move in with her had to be a deliberate and prayerful act. I was mindful that a hasty decision could very well be a costly one. The relationship with my mum was strained since we did not have a strong bond. She had left me in my early childhood in my grandmother's care. She had to do so while seeking employment in New Providence. She never returned to Bannerman Town and moved on with her life without me. Since I had longed for a relationship with my birth mom and wanted her to love me. I jumped at the opportunity to care for her. I secretly longed for a mother-daughter relationship and simultaneously, while nursing my pain, knowing that there was the reality that she might not recover from her illness. During this time, I learned how to bond with my siblings and other relatives I did not know.

I ultimately adjusted to form a bond with my mother. I devoted all of my attention to not only caring for her physical needs but her spiritual needs, too. While my siblings covered the financial expenses. My mother's faith was unshakable. This was a very trying time for the entire family because Mum was the matriarch whose encouragement was the foundation of our family. Despite the doctors' initial adverse reports, Mom rebounded and progressed. We believed that her recovery was built on her trust in the Lord and reading the Bible. The extended three years of her life were based on her church family, relatives, and friends' intercessory prayers. As she was bed-bound, her incapacitated state took a mental toll on each of us.

The mother I developed a relationship with was beautiful, kindhearted, and compassionate. She expressed her love in her actions. Mum would share her love and feelings with me daily. I knew that she was sorry for how she had treated me earlier. The only person I had ever depended on was my grandmother, but now, somehow, the roles were switched. I was dependent upon my mother for my very survival. The reality of this reversed emotional and physical position greatly impacted me. I received the demonstration of 'Love, the kind of love that the Apostle Paul stressed in 1 Corinthians 13:13: "And now these three remain: Faith, Hope, and Love. But the greatest of these is Love". This love message is further reinforced in John 13:18, "Dear children, let us not love with words or speech but with actions and in truth." I grew to love my mother, and eventually, yesteryear's pain was diminished as I allowed my mother's love to invade my heart. Her passion for me dissolved the years of rejection and abandonment.

Ruth equally demonstrated her love for Naomi by not being a financial burden on her mother-in-law. She worked arduously to provide the necessary provision for herself and her mother-in-law. Ruth trusted Naomi's advice and directions concerning in whose field to glean and when to do so. Her being an alien placed a greater demand on her as she was unfamiliar with Jewish customs, traditions, and practices. After successfully gaining the favor of her community, Ruth was challenged to receive kindness rendered and not mistake them for pity.

## DESTINY CROSSROADS/TRUSTING THE SOVEREIGNTY OF GOD IN CHALLENGING TIMES

Ruth could have allowed the challenge of being a foreigner in a strange land to hinder her. Since she trusted her mother-in-law's guidance, she gained the attention of a distant family member who would later become her kinsman-redeemer. With the guidance and love of Naomi, she gained hope and security. The unselfish love between Ruth and Naomi was the catalyst that changed the outcome of an uncertain beginning, eventually producing a triumphant result. When Ruth became Boaz's wife, she brought forth a baby boy, Obed, King David's grandfather. King David, the Giant Killer, wrote many of the Psalms that we frequently quote today. Equally, I was challenged to receive love, and when I opened my heart toward my mother, I received far more than what I had ever expected.

Dear reader, challenges force us to change. Furthermore, social, emotional, and physical challenges alter our perspective on life. Challenges move us from the familiar to the unfamiliar because they bring us into a new sphere of influence. Challenges increase our faith and bring forth hidden blessings, cynicism, and favorable seasons of change. As you read further into my life story, you will see how my bitter challenges turned into sweet fruit.

As I reflected more deeply on the time spent with my mother and the events that had transpired. What should have turned into a nightmare for me, evolved into peaceful life-changing experiences and events. My maternal grandmother's training had prepared me to care for my mother's holistic safety and well-being. Providing clinical attention for me was an easy physical task. Even though the job was emotionally challenging, the experience was bittersweet since we were not truly connected. However, as the days flowed into weeks, the anxiety between us lessened. As we adjusted, the communication between us eventually flowed. As my heart warmed, I became more vocal. My earlier fears, coupled with timidity and rejection, were replaced with confidence as I honestly expressed myself. Despite my being very attentive emotionally, I was reserved most of the time.

On the other hand, my mother was bold in her approach to me. The humility she expressed resulted in my relaxing the hostility I felt. My mother's kindness and humility drew me out of my shell. The awkwardness of being in proximity to my mother soon conceded to relaxation and joy. I wanted to hold on to unforgiveness and remain obstinate. Supernaturally, my mother's love melted and captured my heart in our intimate moments of sharing and caring. I found myself loving the woman whom I had every right to hate. I longed to be with my mother. I wanted to be with her. I resented that she had left me with my grandmother and never looked back. Now, here I was, caring for her and treasuring every moment. This task was unexplainable because caring for my mother was not on the horizon when I left my job. This could only have been the work of my God as he brought me to a "destiny crossroad".

Besides caring for Mum, I also supervised my nieces and nephews after school while my sisters worked at their secular jobs. My duties extended to being a nanny and were another change that I had not anticipated. I sometimes felt extremely uncomfortable having to depend on handouts from family and friends. Their generous financial support brought me to a place of humility. Taking care of my nieces and nephews created countless opportunities for my sisters and me to bond with each other.

Living on the island and being alienated and separated by miles of the ocean did not allow for much interaction with family. Since I had missed out on previous events, I looked forward to family gatherings. They were exciting. The free flow of family in and out of my mother's house encouraged more family gatherings and social interactions. Those occasions provided opportunities to know my loved ones in a more personal and intimate way. I found myself quickly adjusting and moving from outside the circle to becoming an integral part of my siblings' lives. As I am writing this account of my life, I wonder how my life could have perhaps turned out differently if I had never separated from my mother. Nevertheless, being very much aware of my surroundings and my mother's fragile state, I was careful. Rather than inject my insecurities into the conversations and disrupt our gatherings, I kept my feelings to myself.

Those memorable, eventful, and exciting times were undoubtedly no substitute for the lost sections of my life. However, eventually, I learned how to appreciate each meeting, having recognized that each family get-together was a blessing. I decided to live in the moment without allowing past pains to intrude and cloud the present. I chose to forgive. Forgiving my mother for the pain, she had inflicted, maybe unknowingly, on me put me at Destiny's intersection.

I was not forced to forgive; I, however, decided to let go of the past to embrace the present. Turning my back on all the lost family moments and the fact that I did not know my extended family members was another pivotal moment. I concluded in my heart that I could not change the past. I had the power to determine my future, and that is precisely what I did. I wholeheartedly embraced and dived into the family, who accepted me as a part of the clan. We created memories during those family moments, sharing incredible experiences which have transcended long after mum's death.

Altering my mind about my family paved the way for another destiny crossroads moment. I am sure Ruth had a similar experience because she had to contend with leaving Moab behind her to embrace adjusting to life in Bethlehem. Ruth's fight was in her mind. She had to battle with her thoughts, which controlled her feelings. I experienced that freedom begins in the mind. The fruit of emotional and spiritual freedom is first conceived as a thought. *The Bible says, "As a man thinks in his heart, so is he"* (Proverbs 23:7). Ruth's determination and her decision to follow Naomi propelled her forward. As she cut the cord of her past, leaving Moab gave Ruth the courage to embrace the possibility of a new future.

Surprisingly, serving as a caregiver, housekeeper, and nanny brought peace and contentment to my life. The Apostle Paul said, in Philippians 4:11-13. *"Not that I speak in respect of want, for I have learned, in whatsoever state I am, to be content. I know what it is to be in need, and I know what it is to have plenty."* I have learned the secret of being content in any situation, whether well-fed or hungry, whether living in plenty or want. That scripture explained my emotional state and brought much peace as I served my family because I knew that I was fulfilling God's purpose. I was confident that I was in the right place for this moment in time. However, in my mind, I still had an ongoing internal struggle. I was not gainfully employed, and having to rely on others interfered with my independence and self-esteem. Like Ruth, it is hard for an independent individual to receive and accept aid. Often, Christians view support as a favor, while others would label the help pity. I knew that what I was doing was a part of the Lord's plan in my life because the relationship I had gained with my mother was invaluable.

Spiritual and emotional freedom is a personal choice. I decided to protect my mind from negative thoughts and yield my will to Father God. Therefore, when negative thoughts battered my mind, I looked to the Lord rather than giving in to the enemy's lies. Instead, I wrapped myself in the tranquility of I Corinthians 10:5 *"We take hold of every thought and make it obey Christ."* I fought hard to avoid the past thoughts of pain, doubt, fear, insecurity, rejection, self-pity, and uncertainty. When the unpleasant thoughts came creeping around, the warmth of my cloak knitted by the words of I Corinthians 10:5 would insulate and cover me. Because the place in my heart was now filled with love and the old sign of rejection had been exchanged, the new sign hanging on the door of my heart read **'ONLY LOVE RESIDES HERE.'** The Bible was my source of healing. I learned how to apply healing by repeating scripture verses that comforted my mind and spirit.

My precious reader, many individuals find themselves in a similar place as the one I described above. An individual can be saved that is he/she has surrendered his/her life to Jesus, but not all of it because of the refusal to let go of the past. Thus, he/she becomes bound to past situations and or circumstances. On the other hand, some individuals want forgiveness but do not want to forgive. Therefore, unforgiveness becomes a hindrance, preventing a person from experiencing emotional and spiritual freedom. Furthermore, other individuals do not know how to close the door to their past habits, desires, or behaviors and neither do they know what to do when they are bombarded by the flood of negative thoughts that return after they accept Christ.

I need to tell you that accepting Christ does not mean that you will never have another challenge. The Lord knew that we would have challenges because an enemy wants to keep us from having a relationship with Jesus Christ who died so that we might have the power to overcome all challenges, especially those presented by our unseen foe, which is sometimes called the devil, satan, or the enemy. That is why all believers need to understand what it means to accept Christ as their Lord and personal Savior and read their contract or manual, the Bible. My experiences have shown me that only through reading the Bible, worshiping, praying, and fellowshipping with like-minded individuals I can overcome the challenges in my mind.

Connecting with a solid Bible-based church was my source of

strength. My local church's spiritual guidance provided the buffer when my mind was being attacked and flooded with thoughts of past hurt and pain. As you read, my friends, you may be at a *"Destiny Crossroad"* right now. However, it is not the end for you. Just like Ruth, you must be willing to change. If I had not written that initial resignation letter, I would not have had this fantastic opportunity to encourage you

Firstly, change is never easy; however, without making a change, we will remain stagnated. Moving for me meant that I had to grow accustomed to life in the city, which was fast, challenging, and noisy, the extreme opposite of island life, which is tranquil. Secondly, change forced me to think about the reality of my situation. Thinking about my circumstances so often causes me to question my past, present, and future. I reflected many times and wondered if I made the best decision to leave a 20-year career, beloved family, friends, and the tranquility of the island life that I loved so dearly.

Thirdly, I could only imagine what Ruth encountered. Ruth was moving beyond her nation's boundaries and embarking on a cultural exchange that involved her giving up Chemosh's worship, her god, for Israel's God, the Creator of humanity. In other words, Ruth had to make an attitude adjustment, as she was solely dependent on Naomi for her very survival among Bethlehem strangers. Furthermore, can you imagine how humbling it was for Ruth to go to the fields as a worker and pick up leftover grains just to be able to survive? Ruth became a servant to her mother-in-law, a physical role she chose to occupy. She knew what it meant to give herself spiritually to her god, but now Ruth had to yield physically to her mother-in-law, a mortal woman. What a difference! Indeed!

Ruth served Naomi without reservation. She worked and shared her daily experiences with Naomi and found favor in the process. Dear reader, as I end this lengthy chapter on change and challenges, I encourage you to pause and reflect on your life. To experience something you have never embraced before, you must be willing to change.

**D**o you sense a tugging in your spirit that you need to change?

**A**re you afraid of leaving the familiar to embrace the unknown?

**A**re you concerned about what the naysayers will say?

Making a change will put you at the intersection of a "Destiny Crossroad."

Stop and just breathe in! Let me pray for you.

## A Prayer for you!

Sovereign God, I lift the dear reader before you as he/she experiences times of change that he/she will trust in you with all of his/her heart and lean not on his/her understanding, in all ways acknowledge you and you will direct his/her paths. Heavenly Father, I pray the reader will see through the eyes of faith challenges come to make him/her strong and see life in new ways that will transform his/her life and, in turn, be a blessing to those around him/her. Amen

# CHAPTER 3: COURAGE & FAITH

As a Christian, there have been so many scriptures that have guided me through life. Psalms 91 and 23 are two of my favorites. They are such an encouragement because I realized that God was my protector and provider. I trust Him with my life. Ecclesiastes Chapter 3 was another foundational reference that brought me much comfort, reassurance, and peace.

When my mother's doctor gave her the fatal news, we were shocked. The family was heartbroken because we had expected her to be healed. On the other hand, Mom accepted the report bravely and was not interested in seeking further medical advice. Nevertheless, we still trusted God for a miracle. Trusting God's plan meant putting our faith in Him and pressing forward. Romans 8:28 states, *"And we know that for those who love God all things work together for good."* Even though we did not understand God's plan, the family continued to pray for healing.

Even though mom's health began to deteriorate rapidly, she found peace and joy in reading the Bible and singing. We felt helpless as we watched her struggle with losing her ability to function. I did not have the words to describe how I felt as I was the one taking care of her. Mom finally had to be hospitalized. When our family and friends received the news, everyone gathered around her bedside. Her smile was captivating, and even though mom radiated peace, death was near. Despite the doctor's prognosis, I held on to my prayers and trusted that God would heal Mom.

Mother was courageous whenever the doctor spoke to her and did not flinch in her faith in God. She said without blinking, "Gaylean, my faith is in God, and whatever He does is well done." From the day Mom echoed those words, she continued steadfastly and remained resolved in her faith. The Spirit of the Lord surrounded and overshadowed mother.

Everyone who entered her room felt the tangible presence of the Almighty God. I saw a woman who was not afraid to die. After the doctors said they could do nothing else for her, she spent her time on earth encouraging family and friends. I was awed by mom, who was resilient despite her weakness. I still prayed that she would be raised to life as I was not ready for her to depart this world. My heart hurt at the thought of losing mom, and I was overcome with grief. I watched her deteriorate from the jubilant and energetic woman I once knew to a helpless soul. My church family and friends provided solace and comfort to me. I prayed the Word of God over her and encouraged her with the words, "God will see you through." Mom's response was always laced with courage amidst her impending demise.

On February 6th, 2007, she died, while saying these words, "It is well!" Mother passed away peacefully. Watching her die was a beautiful experience. When she passed, my life felt so empty, yet without regret, because I had the extraordinary privilege of taking care of my mother for three years. Besides, if I had not resigned as the Lord instructed me, I would have missed this wonderful bonding with my mom because I was obedient and got to know a beautiful, passionate, and caring woman. Mom was the one who checked every day on family members and planned events and social gatherings.

During my time of grief, the Lord placed 2 Corinthians 1:3-4 at the forefront of my mind. *"Praise be to the God and Father of our Lord Jesus Christ, the Father of compassion and the God of all comfort, who comforts us in all our troubles so that we can comfort those in any trouble with the comfort we received from God."* 2 Corinthians 5:8 became another scripture reference I relied on when I felt depressed, *"We are confident, yes, well pleased, that to be absent from this body is to be present with the Lord."* When mum died, this scripture took on weight because I was assured that she was with the Lord once she died. All her pain and suffering were over, but the agony of her death was hurtful. I had just gotten to know my birth mother, and now she was gone. Even though our time together was short, I felt privileged.

Irrespective of the reassurance of 2 Corinthians 1:3-4, *"Praise be to the God and Father of our Lord Jesus Christ, the Father of compassion and the God of all comfort, who comforts us in all our troubles so that we can comfort those in any trouble with the comfort we received from God."* I honestly did not feel like praising. Repeatedly, I asked myself the question. "How do I move on from the pain of losing my mom?" She was gone. We were connecting so beautifully, worshipping, talking, laughing, and the next time, there was silence. My world was turned upside down. Even though my heart was hurting, I had to be strong because my family leaned on me for strength. What I needed was courage. Unknowingly to those around me, I was silently screaming because I lacked courage and wanted to hide. I did not want to be brave and strong. I just wanted to go into a corner and cry for days.

Mom had become my best friend and confidant. We shared many tender moments and intimate experiences. My heart ached for all the lost seasons and the new memories that we had nurtured in a short period. The last thing I wanted was to be pushed to the forefront and take the lead in planning her funeral. To my surprise, we were comforted when our brother stepped forward to share that mum had left her final wishes with him. Once he shared the details, we all worked together to plan the funeral.

In the Bahamas, funerals are costly events. They are celebrated in style with much pomp, fanfare, and pageantry. Burying a person on the island is equivalent to planning a wedding. Planning a funeral required a considerable amount of time and money. Each funeral usually begins with a 'wake, which is an African tradition handed down from our slave ancestors. The 'wake' is a period of celebration after someone has died. Loved ones and friends would gather to sing, read the Bible, and reflect on the life of the departed. During this occasion, food, drinks, and treats contribute to feeding the family and distribution as people may respect the bereaved family members.

The elaborate funeral service, which could last up to four hours, is also carefully planned to coincide with the departed's final wishes. A drive concludes the church service to the graveyard for a short graveside song service. What happens at the graveside, the final farewell, complements the church service and completes the funeral service. The day ended with an array of food, drinks, and camaraderie. The family greets and fellowships with locals and international relatives who show up to express their love and tell stories and fond memories of the departed. Mom's service was a grand event. The then Prime Minister of our country attended her funeral as my mother was a party supporter. Family and friends flew in from the islands and North America to express their condolences.

After the funeral, I dreaded getting out of bed but gained strength from the well-wishes of the countless people who had loved her. Yes, I read the Bible faithfully, but my heart was heavy since the thought of not seeing mum again was sobering. My mother had become my life. I did not have to think about what we were going to do each day. Like clockwork, we had developed a rhythm. We began each day with thanksgiving and praise.

As I read, mom would listen, reflect and actively discuss the Word of God. I prepared breakfast, lunch, and dinner and administered her medication. I looked forward to bathing and dressing her because I pretended that she was my baby doll. I would chuckle to myself as I selected her daywear. As I massaged her feet, she would wriggle her toes away from me. In the afternoon, before the children came home, I completed the household chores while she was resting.

My weakest point came the day after the funeral, when I went into her room and found her gone. The bed was freshly made, and my best friend was nowhere to be found. That was the day when I realized that she was truly gone. I unashamedly cried aloud for hours, asking Jesus Christ to comfort my heart and give me the courage to accept her death. The first time I had an encounter with courage was the day I left my ex-husband. In the dead of night, I escaped my house and ran with all my might for my life. Using the bright moonlight as a compass, I ran like a sprinter and pushed my battered body to exhaustion. My only goal was to find a haven. I had determined that I had had enough. No more abuse! The courage I experienced that night was supernatural as I had never until that night felt such strength and power to move and say NO.

Honestly, crying out to the Lord in privacy gave me the consciousness to embrace that mom was gone and not returning. I had to continue living. Jesus Christ flooded me again with the supernatural ability and courage to move forward amid my brokenness. Though fearful about what my future would look like, I rebounded and, as the oldest, took charge. By focusing on staying resolute in their presence, I helped my siblings to cope. I temporarily forgot about my fears and galvanized my loved ones to support each other. The courage I received from God also gave me the ability to quiet my inner insecurities. Courage helped me to accept that even in this challenging situation, I would be all right.

Correspondingly, could you imagine the courage it took for Ruth, the Moabite priestess, to leave the temple where she served her God to marry a despised Jewish man? The Bible does not give the details about how a heathen prostitute woman married a respectable Jewish man. Ruth's marriage was unusual because the Jews and the Moabites were rivals who hated each other. This bold act, no doubt, brought her much scrutiny and ridicule. Ruth went against her ethnicity and culture to marry a hated immigrant. Furthermore, she renounced her religion and practices to embrace the faith and beliefs of her husband. They were courageous because they had to defy the odds to be together.

Dear reader, in moments of crisis, it takes faith and courage to move, especially when we anticipate or expect a particular outcome and the opposite happens. Courage gave me the hope I needed to move to the next phase of my life. I held on to the courage to get out of bed each morning. It was only my faith in God that kept me moving from day to day. Sometimes, individuals confuse faith with courage or vice versa. Webster's Dictionary defines faith as complete trust or confidence in someone or something. For example, when I resigned from my job, I was acting in faith. The process was not easy, but I still functioned, believing in faith that the words of my unseen God would come to pass.

On the other hand, courage requires individuals to defy all odds, rise above a difficult situation, keep moving forward and trust what they think they know to bring them through a crisis. Similarly, courage propelled me to leave my home and move to the city despite the fear I felt. I am so thankful that I was able to lean on the strength of God's Word. I had the Bible and the peace that came from reading and worshipping Jesus. I do not know how individuals cope when they do not have a relationship with Jesus Christ.

According to Bible commentary, as a widow, Ruth had to wrestle with courage and faith. Based on her mother-in-law's advice, she agreed to pursue a man on the threshing floor to receive an offer of marriage. Naomi and Ruth were destitute, and because of Naomi's interference, Ruth found favor with Boaz, who was Naomi's relative. When Naomi suggested that Ruth meet Boaz on the threshing floor at night to seek his protection, the move was bold and unorthodox. Jewish women did not pursue men; hence, Ruth's agreement to break Jewish tradition took courage. It was a move of desperation because they were both hopeless.

As mentioned in the Bible, the threshing floor was where farmers would separate the wheat from the grain. Moreover, on the night in question, Boaz was eating and drinking with his comrades and male servants. That day's culture suggests that Ruth could have been stoned or perhaps banished from Bethlehem, Judah if she was seen at night on or near the threshing floor, a place reserved only for the men. Naomi was aware of the stakes, and she knew that going to the threshing floor as a single woman was risky. I believe that their desperate situation caused both to be reckless in their decisions.

Moreover, I could only imagine the courage it took knowing that the outcome could be fatal to defy Jewish tradition. It took great courage for Naomi to ask Ruth to risk her life, and it took even more courage and faith to believe that, despite the odds, she could succeed. Ruth trusted her mother-in-law. Dressed in boldness and confidence, she went to the threshing floor to have an encounter with Boaz.

Ruth laid at the feet of Boaz, that traditional act of submission announcing her willingness to humble herself and be obedient to the advice of Naomi. Ruth expressed her submission to Boaz. That was a priceless moment of trust. However, in doing so, Ruth took a significant risk because she had no idea whether or not Boaz would accept her. At his feet, she was restored, and her self-worth was redeemed. Boaz was willing to pay her bride price. Even though they met in secret, Ruth felt encouraged that she was worthy of love. Her bold move of submission and reverence displayed at the feet of Boaz was unprecedented.

Ruth was rewarded and gained protection, security, and a marriage proposal from her kinsman-redeemer. Reader, there are times in life when I have learned that people must be prepared to do what they have never done before to receive something they had never received. Taking a risk of this magnitude can only be undertaken when courage intersects with faith. I was about to experience another *"Destiny Crossroads" encounter.* I was about to step into deeper waters as the pain of losing mum consumed my life.

Before Mom's death, my daughters had spoken to me about joining them in North America; however, I was reluctant. Eventually gaining the courage to make the bold decision to leave the Bahamas. I consented to their request and, deciding to leave the Bahamas, placed me at another intersection with *"Destiny Crossroads."* This time moving took more courage and an extra measure of faith.

Making the shift meant leaving my country, friends, and family behind to embrace unfamiliar territory. At this interval, I felt just like Ruth. I was still very emotional and heavy-hearted as I struggled with whether I wanted to give up the familiar comfort in exchange for another life experience. "*Destiny Crossroad*" was once again pushing me towards another connection with the unknown. This crossing would stretch my faith even more than before. I was now uncertain about starting over again since I was still hurting. I knew something was wrong, but I did not know how to fix the problem. I was being tormented by grief and needed healing. I began praying and asking the Lord to heal me from grief's clutches.

As faith would have it, healing flowed as they embraced me when I arrived in America and reunited with my daughters. I cried and laughed. It was the release of those emotions that caused the supernatural power of healing to invade my heart. The love of my daughters and their joyful welcoming presence drove the spirit of grief away. The sadness and despair that clouded my heart and mind gradually dissolved as I spent weeks and months meditating on the verses below. These scriptural nugget verses helped me lift my head and move forward to embrace what was ahead.

## Trusting God's Sovereignty in All Things - Romans 8:28

And we know that in all things,

God works for the good of those who love him, who has been called according to his purpose?

NIV: New International Version

## Faith Never Fails - 2nd Corinthians 5:7

For we live by faith, not by sight.

NIV: New International Version

Now faith is confidence in what we hope for and assurance about what we do not see.

NIV: New International Version

## Mental Toughness to Persevere - Philippians 4:13

I can do all this through him who gives me strength.

NIV: New International Version

..........................

## My Prayer for You

Heavenly Father, I ask that you inspire the individual praying this prayer right now in the name of your son Jesus Christ.

I pray that his/her faith will not fail Jesus gives them the courage and faith to move forward through every situation.

Father God infuses each person with the knowledge and awareness that nothing is impossible when he/she believes.

I speak over him/her now that all things are working out for his/her good, according to your plans for his/her life.

Fill him/her now with Your peace in Jesus' name, Amen.

# CHAPTER 4: WHEN DESTINY CALLS

According to Merriam-Webster's Dictionary, a decision is a choice one must make after arriving at a conclusion or considering a series of events. A decision should often be followed by promptness and firmness in fulfilling a specific cause of action. Deciding to relocate to the United States was naturally fearful. What I did not know at that time was that my movements were supernatural and divinely orchestrated by the Lord. I have learned that even in fear or during fearful situations, I must obey the Master. Relocating was a *"Destiny Crossroads"* moment.

The transition was critical, as the stakes were high because there was a possibility that I could potentially be stopped and not allowed to enter Florida. My visitor's visa only allowed me a six-month stay in the U.S.A. I knew that this move was a permanent one; however, I did not know when I would achieve residency status. At the time, only one of my daughters was an American resident, and the other was in the process of filing her paperwork.

Despite being overwhelmed with clouds of doubt, I left the Bahamas in 2007 with my possessions, consisting of two medium-sized bags, my Bible, and precious pictures and letters from my family and friends. I walked away from all that was familiar, including all of my earthly treasures and valuable possessions. Just like Ruth, I was turning my back on what was comfortable to launch into the unknown. I must admit that during this process, fear bombarded my thoughts, and fear was always knocking at the door of my heart and my mind. Fear bombarded my mind with projections of doubt and failure. However, God, through His love and grace, counteracted fear, neglect, and doubt with Psalms 34:4, "I sought the Lord, and He answered me; He delivered me from all my fears." This scripture became my mantra and walking stick; whenever I faltered, I would quote it to soothe my mind and calm my spirit. I had to believe the spoken and written Word of God. I choose to believe that the Lord Jesus Christ would open supernatural doors and provide tangible opportunities for success for me.

When I decided to move, I was fully aware that the American natural laws were against my staying on a tourist visa, and there might be consequences, such as deportation and or having my visa canceled. However, I was operating in crazy faith, knowing that I had heard the voice of the Lord telling me to go to America. Dear friend, Hebrews 11:1 describes faith as the substances of things hoped for and the evidence of things unseen. Faith is a supernatural empowerment given by the Holy Spirit to a believer to perform a function or complete an assignment. Likewise, Christians refer to crazy faith as knowing that what they see or are about to embark upon is impossible and can only become possible with the divine intervention of Jesus Christ. Now, the crazy portion is when an individual decides to believe that the impossible can become possible no matter how long it takes. For faith to be fully experienced, we must live, learn, love, listen, persevere, and overcome.

Although I was doubtful at times, I was convinced that I had heard the voice of God telling me to pack my bags. Despite what my family and friends were telling me, I made my plans. I was functioning in a power that I could not explain in words. I was convinced that the Holy Spirit told me to move and that I would be successful, so I obeyed. Furthermore, if I had concentrated on my six-month visa, I would have never moved because I was a law-abiding citizen. The Bible says, "The Lord has not given us a spirit of fear but one of love, power and a sound mind. This scripture can be found in II Timothy 1:7. God has given every believer the ability to operate in faith. Faith is the currency of heaven; faith moves God, and without faith, it is impossible to please the Father (Hebrews 11:6).

On the other hand, the enemy of faith is doubt. Disbelief and doubt are the by-products of fear. The voice of doubt and unbelief tag-team to cripple, hinder and delay believers from obeying the Word and the voice of Father God. The duo of doubt and unbelief form the stronghold known as fear in mind. Fear is the root that produces unbelief and doubt. These three works together to continuously prevent believers from advancing and fulfilling the work of the Kingdom. Rest assured that whenever an individual is fearful, there is always evidence of doubt and unbelief in that person's life.

For further clarity, a stronghold is like a castle, a fortified structure that can withstand pressure and penetration from all external forces. The concrete exterior is sturdy so that nothing can penetrate or infiltrate the perimeter of the castle. A stronghold or castle is a thought or thoughts that a person struggles back and forth within the mind. Fear is a stronghold that seeks to cripple and paralyze a person from moving forward. When its tentacles wrap around the mind, the venom of doubt and unbelief is released into an individual's heart. Fear does not discriminate, nor does it respect origin or ethnicity. Fear torments and reduces its victims like infants. Once the claws of fear grip a person, they cage the mind and heart and prevent that person from advancing. Moreover, the only outcomes that one can envision are doom and gloom. That is how fear operates in the life of an individual.

Not being a legal resident in the U.S.A. was fear manifested in my life in many ways, but especially when out in public. Firstly, I feared that Custom Border Patrol officials would pick me up. Secondly, I was doubtful about my ability to adjust to a new culture. Repeatedly, I asked myself if I could adapt to the freedom and candidness of the culture. With much caution, I slowly learned how to acclimatize to my new environment. My dialect also challenged me because certain words I used were not understood. This resulted in my repeating myself. At times, I became frustrated and would shut down, resolving never to speak again. However, I eventually realized that living in another culture came with its prescribed challenges, which were not unique. Rather than expect others to adjust to me, I changed my attitude and tried to speak more slowly to be understood.

That was the beginning of a transformation for me. My daughter also took the time to expose me to the social graces and protocols needed to assimilate into this new culture and environment in which I lived. With her help, I was able to overcome my earlier fears, anxieties, and frustrations. Dear reader, I do not encourage you to move to a new country without procuring legal status before migrating. The opportunity to obtain residency was a priority for me because my daughter was already a legal resident. Although obeying God's Word is never easy, the Lord will provide the grace to endure hardships.

Once we obey the Lord, His grace and mercy will lead us to success and destiny fulfillment. I was always mindful and comforted by how Ruth acted at her *"Destiny Crossroads"* moment, when she said to Naomi, "do not charge me to leave you or turn back from you, where you go, I will go, and where you stay, I will stay, your people will be my people and your God my God." Ruth's words shaped and fulfilled her prophetic destiny. Her future (**Destiny**) was shaped by the words she spoke; Proverbs 18:21 declares, "the tongue has the power of life and death, and those who love it will eat its fruit." I believe Ruth released those words without fully understanding the outcome. In choosing to leave Moab with her mother-in-law, she gave up everything familiar surrounding her gods, country, family, culture, and friends. Ruth's bold and determined decision thrust her into fulfilling god's divine purpose and destiny for her life.

Dear reader, the decisions we make today affect not only us at our moment of a crossroads but also our future generations. Ruth's name is mentioned in the genealogy of Jesus, Matthew 1:5. We look it up and read it for ourselves. Ruth, a Moabite priestess and a heathen woman, is listed in the Bible as being connected to Jesus. WOW!

Ruth could have turned back, but she decided to move forward. I have learned from my own experiences that when God's sovereign hand is upon your life, the choices you make might appear foolish to other people. However, each segment of your life eventually aligns with His purpose and plan for your life. Leaving my beloved country, the Bahamas, was all in the plan of God for my life. It did not matter who thought I had missed God; I knew that moving to America was the divine will of God for my life.

If you are tired of asking questions and wondering when and if your situation will change, say the prayer below and ask the Lord to speak to your heart, giving you directions and clarity concerning the next decision regarding your future that you must make.

Read the prayer quietly in your heart and only pray it out aloud if you are willing to respond to the voice of destiny. Don't say the prayer because I ask you to do so, but instead say it because that is what you desire in your heart.

## My Prayer for You

Heavenly Father, I pray that your divine insight and protection would guide me into my predestined place.

Jesus, I want to hear from you when you speak to me.

Lord, give me the courage and desire to follow your voice and not allow doubt and unbelief to prevent me from obeying you when you speak to my heart.

I pray that, just like Gaylean and Ruth, I will experience your hand in my life as I learn how to hear you and obey your instructions. Jesus, teach me your Word and give me the capacity to remember scripture verses so that when fear, doubt, and unbelief come knocking at the door of my heart. I can use your Word, the Bible, as my defense.

I want to know you, Lord, in your fullness. I am tired of making my own decisions,
I want to know your plans for my life. And surrender my life fully to you.
Lord, I give up, and I trust you with my life. Let your kingdom come, and you will be done in me.

Amen

After you say the prayer, play the song "I give my life fully committed to you." https://www.youtube.com/watch?v=PYInYloXrR4

# CHAPTER 5: MOVING FORWARD IN FAITH

Webster's dictionary defines faith as "the firm belief of something to which there is no proof." Many people talk about faith, but in my own experience, very few are able to provide proof of faith. For example, I had to credit supplies, but because I knew that I would receive monies at the end of the month, I was comfortable knowing that I could credit goods. I would often say to my colleagues that I was living by faith. I certainly thought that I was crediting against monies that I had not earned as yet.

One might argue that it took faith to establish credit. I, however, would like to say that my actions were not a result of faith. Knowing that I would receive a salary provided a cushion and mental comfort that I would have the cash to cover the credited amount. In my life, I worked faith from the angle that faith was believing in what I could not see now. In the past, that formula worked for me. Still, once I relocated to America, I was about to be tested on an entirely different level.

According to Hebrews 11:1, "Faith is hoping in something you cannot see but acting like you know it exists until it manifests." I quoted this verse on numerous occasions, but like my example indicated above, I never embraced the Bible's faith because I always had a cushion, which is something that we rely upon to rescue us from a challenge or crisis. Family, friends, credit cards, or bank loans are all types of cushions. Once I accessed this network, the incorporation of these resources nullified the Bible's definition of faith. Trusting my network ultimately brought me through every situation; however, could I honestly say that I had relied on God? I would further argue that someone reading this chapter would say that perhaps God allowed the network to provide the needed assistance. That is debatable, and you can ultimately decide for yourself once you have read this chapter.

In the beginning, when my adventure became a reality, I panicked. I came to the USA with only $300 and two suitcases. How was I going to survive without a job or a steady income? I had no other source of income other than my daughter. Even though I lived with my daughter, it was not her responsibility to take care of me. The $300.00 did not last a week. Although my daughter was employed, as a single mom with rent, car payments, and other bills, she was not in a good financial position to fully care for me.

Whatever she had, we made it work. God provided for us supernaturally. This is the only way I can describe how it all happened.

"Therefore, I tell you, do not worry about your life, what you will eat or drink; or about your body, what you will wear. Is not life more than food and the body more than clothes? Look at the birds of the air; they do not sow or reap or store away in barns, and yet your heavenly Father feeds them. Are you not much more valuable than they? Can any one of you, by worrying, add a single hour to your life? "And why do you worry about clothes? See how the flowers of the field grow. They do not labor or spin. Yet I tell you that not even Solomon in all his splendor was dressed like one of these. If that is how God clothes the grass of the field, which is here today and tomorrow is thrown into the fire, will he not much more clothe you—you of little faith? So do not worry, saying, 'What shall we eat?' or 'What shall we drink?' or 'What shall we wear?' For the pagans run after all these things, and your heavenly Father knows that you need them. But seek first his kingdom and his righteousness, and all these things will be given to you as well. Therefore, do not worry about tomorrow, for tomorrow will worry about itself. Each day has enough trouble of its own." Matthew 6:25-34 NIV

Living by faith would challenge me financially. I could think about a few occasions when supernatural faith was extended to my daughter and me. A few times when the rent was due, and we did not have the full amount, the rental manager would extend the deadline. When the car payment was delinquent and almost up for repossession, we did not know what would happen. Once we prayed, negative decisions would be overturned in our favor.

One night, we had not a morsel of food in our cupboard. We did not know what we were going to eat the next day. In desperation, I went onto the balcony and prayed, asking God to provide food. My mom's death and my decision to leave the Bahamas had placed a wedge between my sisters and me, and therefore, I could not call home for help. In faith, I prayed, asking and trusting that He would provide and take away these adverse circumstances. No more than thirty minutes after praying, my daughter received a phone call from a coworker who did not know our situation. By the end of the night, we had more than $200.00 worth of groceries.

Occasionally, a few of my close friends from home would spontaneously send me a small monetary gift that I allowed to accumulate. I would use those funds to purchase my personal needs. Let me say that their gifts were not regular, yet I treasured their generosity. I would thank them for their offerings. I also had a friend on the East Coast who would send me to assist her in her home and would thank me by giving me a stipend. There were also times when we needed to travel, and there was no gas in the car. I prayed that a miracle would occur in many ways.

During those lean days, the more I prayed, the more God provided for our needs. Money would appear in my account, and I kept praying. Eventually, my daughter applied for another job. We prayed that she would get the job, and she was offered it. Her income significantly increased to the point where she could pay off her car note. Later, when my second daughter began working in the army, she would regularly send me funds.

When I was asked to speak at an event, many times I had no means of getting to the venue. I prayed that someone from the Bahamas would call me, and before I was required to travel, I had more than enough to secure my passage to the event. I also enrolled in a Bible course with a firm conviction that the Lord had instructed me to do so. Every time I signed up in faith, each class was paid for in full. I earned more than ten certificates in Biblical studies from credible institutions.

I learned how to walk in faith by experiencing faith. Faith has become my lifestyle, and even as I write this chapter, I stand amazed at Jesus Christ. I desired to have a car to embrace the work of missions freely and have the freedom to move when I wanted to, so I prayed for a car. To date, I have an automobile that was given to me. A lady at my church walked up to me and said, "I feel like I need to bless you with my car." I have a reliable, comfortable, stylish car, and I owe it all to my faith in God, my miracle worker!

God loves you, dear reader. I pray that Jehovah Jireh, the Lord who provides, will supply all your needs according to your faith. He has a perfect plan for your life. Only believe. Faith in God requires action! It took faith for Ruth to move to Bethlehem, Judah. Even though her faith did not directly involve finances, she had to exercise faith because she believed Naomi's words. Ruth placed her life in the stories her mother-in-law spoke concerning a place she had never visited. Later, she had to have faith to believe that if she followed the reapers, she would gather enough grain or food for Naomi and her. Following that, her faith in Naomi's directions caused her to gain the attention of a wealthy man who later became her husband. Furthermore, Ruth's faith placed her among the Bible hallmarks as she is recorded in the lineage of Jesus Christ.

Faith transitioned a heathen woman into the Jewish Torah. Ruth's faith required her to be obedient. Well, the ingredient of obedience activates faith, and her faith demonstrated that anything is possible when we put our faith in God. Faith erases the impossible and makes the intangible tangible. Faith in God brings the unseen into the present! Faith causes our words to become a reality. Faith gives a believer hope to trust in an unseen God.

Are you ready to be **BOLD AND WALK IN FAITH**?

Are you ready to **GET UP AND MOVE**?

Are you prepared to **PUSH AGAINST THE ODDS**?

Are you willing to **PUT YOUR FAITH IN GOD**?

# Prayer

Ask the Lord to help you, and He will give you the faith and confidence to move forward.

# CHAPTER 6: JOY AND NEWNESS

When I arrived in America, I was met by my two daughters, who had been legally living in the USA for several years. I noticed the excitement on their faces, and I immediately assumed that they were happy because I had arrived! To my surprise, my youngest daughter said, "Mom, you are going to be a grandmother. My sister is pregnant." I, however, noticed the apprehension in her voice; the news was both shocking and exciting. I was going to be a grandmother! During the ride to our destination, the conversation was centered on the news of the pregnancy.

I was at a "Destiny Crossroads." I had to choose to accept my daughter's pregnancy or reject her news because of her being unmarried. It was morally and socially unacceptable for an unmarried young woman to have a child. In the Bahamas, due to the underlining social pressure, ladies would prefer to abort a child rather than give birth. The spiritual pressure was unimaginable, however, the stigma attached to one's family was even more significant. As an elder in my church, I had to decide whether to accept and support my daughter or reject her because her mistake was visible to the world. The thoughts were fleeting as they caressed my mind, but they were overpowered by the thoughts of my being a grandmother. I chose to embrace the comforting feeling of consuming my being. Feelings of excitement and joy flood my heart, and I made it known to my children that I was happy.

Weeks later, I found a home church, and it was difficult for me to acclimate because I was the only foreigner in the congregation. In the beginning, while interacting with people, I felt awkward because of my thick, unique, and broad Bahamian accent. Feelings of intimidation overwhelmed me. I found myself, on many occasions, withdrawing and shutting down. Nevertheless, I continued to attend church because I needed to hear the Word of God and serve others. As I continued to participate in the church, I adjusted to being different. During the course of interacting with my new spiritual family, I was aware that many of the people in my new church had never been exposed to ethnic differences.

Therefore, I made it a point of encouraging them to come out of their safe spaces and embrace other cultures. While learning to navigate those differences, I expanded and enjoyed my new experiences while growing in my faith and learning to love my congregation. While I was learning how to navigate my new environment and culture, my life was shifted by my grandson's birth.

On November 05th, 2008, I witnessed the birth of my first grandchild, a baby boy, welcomed into the world. I was allowed to cut his umbilical cord. It was an honor. My heart melted, and I exhaled. All of the feelings of pain ceased to exist; the shackles around my heart and mind fell off. I was free! The hole in my heart instantaneously disappeared. Love consumed me from my head to my toe. My precious gift, my new grandbaby, took center stage. Nothing else mattered. The baby brought me so much joy and excitement. I became his nanny. Taking care of him was my sole purpose.

My grandson occupied my day, and caring for him helped me let go of my mother, thus speeding up the grieving process. God is amazing in how He manifests His goodness and His love toward us. I was so blessed to watch the different stages of my grandson's growth and development; I enjoyed every precious moment right up until the time he began school.

Watching my grandson develop daily was so comforting to me. When he began school at three years old, I was normal again, so I focused all of my attention on my church responsibilities. To keep myself busy, I enrolled in in-house classes on various religious topics that I enjoyed. I was also involved in evangelistic outreaches around the city. My world was rapidly changing from taking care of a newborn grandson to meeting and embracing new friends and acquaintances to exploring a new town. Like Ruth, who was willing to adapt to a new culture, I was doing likewise. Ruth's journey was one of hope and expectancy, and I was following in her footsteps. As a foreigner, I felt so out of place at times, but I never regretted leaving the Bahamas. It was my choice.

I was, however, unaware that I was about to have another encounter with "Destiny Crossroads.". A global missionary visited and spoke at my church. As I listened intently, I felt a stirring in my spirit toward evangelism. Memories of life in the Bahamas filled my mind. My grandmother on the island of Eleuthera always housed the missionaries who came to the island. They lived with us. As I reminisced, more memories flooded my mind about a missionary named Mother Willimae Eloise Davis Wilson, who was from Cat Island, one of the islands in the Bahamas. Mother Wilson was affectionately called "mother" by my grandmother. Her smile, features, and beautiful, sweet personality were unforgettable. When it was time for the missionary to leave our house, I wept bitterly in disappointment that she had to leave us. The missionary lady did her best to console me by telling me that I would be all right.

As I sat pondering that incident, I believed that it was at that moment I received a spiritual impartation for missions. Serving the less fortunate and helping in outreach and evangelism have always been the areas that I would gravitate towards in the church. However, until that point, I had never stopped to wonder why. This message deeply touched my heart. When I left church that night, I felt a longing for the mission field in my heart. Fulfilling the call to mission was way beyond my ability. I had no idea how this mission would happen.

Missions are a vocation or calling of a religious organization, especially Christianity, when persons go out into the world and spread their faith. Years before immigrating to the USA, I had several dreams about living in a foreign country. I thought it was just a dream and never imagined that years later, my dreams would become a reality. Dear reader, what is it that you have longed to do or become as a child growing up? Can you still remember your dream? Is the dream still alive in your heart? It is not too late, as nothing is impossible if you believe. If you can see your vision, you can give birth to your dream.

## Prayer

Heavenly Father, I declare over the reader that every dream and vision that has been in his/her heart as a child or even later in life will no longer just be a dream, but it will become a reality. Believe, never give up on yourself.

Heavenly Father, I pray that the reader will be encouraged to embrace the new changes taking place in his/her life right now and trust in your sovereignty to see him/her through.

## CHAPTER 7: WALKING IN FAVOR

After the mission session ended, I was even more consumed with the possibility of serving as an overseas missionary. This conference only served to further stimulate my desire for the work of evangelism. To my delight, in 2010, I was presented with an opportunity to go on a mission trip to Burkina Faso, West Africa. I was thrilled about the possibility of serving as an overseas missionary.

Despite my lack of finances, I prayed that I would be the individual chosen by my pastor to represent our church district. Amidst my excitement, I was mindful that since my papers were currently being processed, if I left the country before they were finalized according to Immigration Law, it would result in deportation. Although knowing this fact, my love for missions and the likelihood of going to Africa consumed my heart, pushing out the natural law of human reasoning.

I was excited as I was about to live my dream of finally serving in a foreign country. Even before I received the official decision about the trip, in faith, I began sharing with my family and some close friends that I was going on a mission trip. Everyone was so excited as they all knew how much I loved people and embraced every opportunity to serve. When I received the call from my pastor, I was not surprised but humbled that I was selected to serve and represent the ministry. I was going to West Africa! Before traveling, I had to complete a two-week training with the mission agency to be certified to share the Gospel. I received extensive in-depth training about the culture and ethnicity of sharing the Bible in the Eastern part of the world.

There was so much to learn about the French-speaking province of Burkina Faso, West Africa. Each tribe in Africa has its own distinct traditions. There was much to learn. The training was intense, and I absorbed the new information with vigor as my love for the mission field expanded. My ten-week trip to Burkina Faso, West Africa, was an adventurous journey of faith and favor.

Similarly, I believe that Ruth had much to learn as she was immersed in the Judaean culture. Ruth chose to embrace a new culture with her mother-in-law without knowing what to expect. On the other hand, I was compelled to go to Africa by the supernatural prompting of Father

# DESTINY CROSSROADS/TRUSTING THE SOVEREIGNTY OF GOD IN CHALLENGING TIMES

God. Unfamiliar with the Eastern world, I absorbed everything that I was taught. My daughter had submitted the paperwork to apply for my residency months prior. Hence, I was prohibited from leaving the country. Notwithstanding this, I felt a pressing need in my spirit to obey God as the children of Africa were calling my name. After much prayer, I knew that I had to move on with my plans to leave the country. I believed that God was going before me, and I was determined to obey him. My daughters were very concerned and fearful that my going on this trip would interrupt the process of finalizing my residency.

My church family and friends helped to raise the finances needed for my ticket and living expenses. The team was comprised of eight individuals; I was the only one chosen from Florida to attend. Weeks before departure, everyone except me had purchased their tickets because the deadline was quickly approaching. Our American host in Burkina Faso was very concerned that I had not bought my ticket. The likelihood that my reservations would be canceled was a genuine possibility. There was nothing that I could have done because I did not have the available funds to purchase it. I continued to speak words of faith, confessing that I was going on that trip. A week later, a couple paid my fare and provided additional funds as a bonus. The Lord did provide!

Dear reader, I encourage you to believe that nothing is impossible with God. You can fulfill and accomplish all that you desire once you put God first. No matter the challenge, see yourself as the winner by visualizing the finish line. Trust God. Never Give Up! All athletes who desire to win their sporting event must exercise discipline and train continuously. The vision of the prize causes them to push despite their mental and physical discomfort.

The mental and physical resolve to never give up causes an athlete to achieve a favorable outcome. It is the same way in the spiritual. If we love God and have the desire to obey His word, we will reap a reward. Similarly, we exercise by fasting, praying, reading, worshipping, declaring, and meditating on the word of God. Engaging in these daily activities will cause an individual to build spiritual muscles. As individuals continue with these spiritual activities, they will grow spiritually, and their belief in God will expand. Eventually, they will receive the answer to what they were believing. When we do our part, God will reward us for our obedience. Faith in God will be richly rewarded, and the word of God will work for our good. I am a living witness, and I have countless testimonies that faith in God produces results.

Deep within my soul, I knew that God had provided the opportunity for me to go to Africa, and as a result, I was confident that Jesus Christ would provide the finances. Friends, I did not have the hundreds of dollars that I needed to fund the trip, but I had faith. Based on the Bible, my faith surely produced favor.

On September 30th, 2010, I boarded a flight for a long journey to Ouagadougou airport in Burkina Faso, West Africa. I departed from Florida and then traveled to Paris, where we connected with the rest of the mission team. During the six-hour flight to Africa, I was excited. For the first time, I allowed myself to think about Africa and how I would adjust to life in a village with limited amenities. The idea of learning how to communicate in French caused me great anxiety.

When we arrived in Burkina Faso, the heat was unbearable. On exiting the aircraft, I walked very quickly into the terminal building to escape the heat. The hot, dry African weather embraced me like a glove. The heat was so intense that no training could have prepared my body for the scorching temperature. Within minutes, we were met by our host and escorted to our destination. As we drove through the town, I experienced a cultural shock. Burkina Faso was vastly different from the United States and the Bahamas. In most areas, the infrastructure was lacking. The vehicular traffic was chaotic as there was no systematic order to the traffic flow. I was afraid that an accident would happen.

To forget about the traffic and the arid temperature, I envisioned how the children would look and what they would say on our arrival. My passion for the children allowed me to see beyond the unfamiliar road traffic, which consisted of animals, cars, buses, and motorbikes driving at an alarming speed.

When we arrived at our destination, we were briefed on what to expect for our ten-week assignment. The native language of Burkina Faso is French. On the first day, with the local missionaries, we began with a crash course in French. Although we had a wonderful teacher, learning French was a significant challenge. I struggled to grasp the pronunciation of the language. Praising the Lord with the Holy Spirit's help and the young people on the team, I was able to speak using basic greetings and introductory phrases. Adjusting to village life reminded me of living on the island. I felt at home because of the food, and the friendliness of the people reminded me of the Bahamian way of life.

I was pleasantly surprised to discover a sugar apple fruit tree that was native to my country. I was shocked as I never expected to have some of the similar foods and treats with which I was familiar. Also, I met a village elder who shared with me aspects of my Bahamian ancestors. I was aware that my ancestors were slaves who came to the Bahamas because of the slave trade, but I did not know from which area of Africa they had come. Many slaves who were prisoners of war were either released by the British privateers in the Bahamas or slaves of the Loyalists who settled in the Bahamas.

Life in Burkina Faso was an adventure as the kids were our focus, and we spent most of our time ministering to them. Another aspect of our ministry team was to help in building water wells to provide better drinking water for residents. The most challenging part of the mission work was witnessing the suffering of human beings. Poverty was due to a hopeless mindset at this time. The training I received before traveling was of paramount importance as it helped me to see beyond poverty and to remain focused on the children. The puppet ministry was indeed a blessing for us on this mission.

Our team brought much joy and encouragement to not only the kids but also the older people in the village. Every day, the smiling faces of the children filled my heart with joy and contentment. Watching the children learn new ideas and information was such a blessing. They were excited and welcomed us with open arms. The Puppet ministry and sharing the Word of God brought hope to the children; as they told others about the ministry every day, the number multiplied. They looked forward to hearing us speak their language and telling stories about a God they did not know. Even though I missed my grandson, daughters, church family, friends, and relatives, I knew I was in the right place, doing what I dreamed about as a child. Our work was appreciated. The time passed very quickly since every day was filled with activity.

During my work ministering to the villagers, I was simultaneously very concerned and prayerful about my re-entry into the USA. I had spoken to the team about my dilemma, and as a result, they were praying that I would not have an issue regarding my re-entering the USA. We prayed for God's Divine favor. Every time I would mention my concerns to the team, I was given words of reassurance and comfort. The scripture that I held on to was Romans 8:28, "and we know that in all things work for the good of those who love God and have been called according to his purpose." I knew that my life was in God's hands. I believed and trusted Him because I was doing what He asked me to do. His presence was going ahead to ensure that everything would be favorable with immigration at the border.

I had fallen in love with the children and the natives, so when the time came to say goodbye, I was sad. I was overly emotional because I wished I could have taken some of the children home with me. My heart was so consumed with leaving them behind that I was momentarily distracted from my pressing issue. I cried until we arrived at the airport. My tears caused me to dispel my apprehension about re-entering the United States and renewed my confidence in God. I believed that because I trusted Him, I would receive favor. I had learned that words, whether positive or negative, were potent and powerful, as God has given us, His children, the power to speak life and death. The words we speak will produce positive or negative results.

Ruth exemplifies this when her mother-in-law Naomi encouraged her to return home. Ruth told Naomi that she would live wherever she lived and that her people and your God would be Ruth's people and her God. Ruth's words produced life. She left Moab and experienced life in Naomi's house and life in Boaz's field, which provided food and sustenance. Ruth also experienced life by heeding Naomi's voice in meeting Boaz on the threshing floor, receiving a marriage proposal, following Naomi's words, and obeying Naomi's words through the birth of her son, Obed. Do you know that Ruth is mentioned in the genealogy of Jesus Christ?

What Ruth said placed her in the Hallmark of Jewish history. Through her marriage to Boaz, she was grafted into the lineage of Jesus Christ. In desperation, she uttered, "I would live wherever you live. Your people and your God will be my people and my God." Through speaking these words, Ruth changed her destiny.

# DESTINY CROSSROADS/TRUSTING THE SOVEREIGNTY OF GOD IN CHALLENGING TIMES

Dear reader, I want to ask you a few questions, but I do not expect you to have a ready answer. I, however, want you to ponder your responses before answering my questions. How you respond to these questions can change the trajectory of your life.

- **What** are you speaking about?

- **What** words are you allowing to come out of your mouth?

- **Do** you know that you were created to speak?

- **Do** you know that the words you release can create a negative or positive outcome?

- **Do** you know that you can change and shape your destiny by speaking what God has said about you?

- **Do** you see yourself as a winner over life's setbacks or disappointments?

- **What** are you prepared to do to change your future?

- **Do** you know that the Bible says that faith without works is dead? Ruth's faith and words produced favor in her life.

- **Do** you know that you can also experience favor by speaking what the Bible has spoken concerning you?

I challenge you to begin searching the scriptures and find out what God has spoken concerning your life. Open your mouth and loudly speak or listen to yourself reading the Bible. Continue speaking until you see a result, no matter how long it takes. If you do not give up, you will experience manifestation. The words you speak will materialize. Favor is knocking at your door. Answer the door with the words you speak!

# CHAPTER 8: THE OUTCOME

On December 14th, 2010, I arrived at Newark Liberty Airport, New Jersey. This was my first solo entry into the U.S.A. At the Customs checkpoint. I cordially greeted the Immigration officer. When was the last time you were in America? I responded truthfully. He looked at me without a word, closed my passport, and began working on his computer.

Afterward, he called another officer over to his desk. The officer with a gun attached to his right side came forward and told me to follow him. As I followed him, I prayed, "God, you are bigger than these guys." He took me to a detention room and politely told me to have a seat. Being afraid, I still held my composure and tried to relax. I was detained, without knowing what the outcome would be. My connecting flight to Florida was leaving in two hours, and yet I had not checked in.

When my name was called, I approached the counter. The officer asked me the same questions as the earlier officer had done. I again responded truthfully. I then asked for permission to supply a further explanation. I explained that my daughter had submitted my papers for legal residency before I left the country with the mission team. My fears were dispelled when the officer said to me in the middle of my explanation, "Relax! Everything is going to be all right!" Peace flooded my entire being as he took me into his private office and permitted me to call my daughter to explain the situation. He then later began the four-hour computer process to readmit me into the country. The wait was tiring but peaceful. Glory be to God; I had just experienced outcome #1.

I was questioned again about what I was doing in Africa. As I spoke about the mission trip, the response I received was, "Okay, you were doing great work." The favor was on my side. I kept thanking God in my heart for the blessing I was receiving from the Customs officials. Since my original flight had departed, an airline representative brought me a new departure schedule, a boarding pass, and my luggage. Hallelujah, outcome #2 was just handed to me.

When the re-entry process was completed, I was released to venture to the departure gate and await my flight to Florida. As I was departing the detention area, one of the officers said to me, "We were supposed to deport you out of this country for ten years." Glory be to God, outcome #3. I nodded my head in acknowledgment of his words. In my heart, I was rejoicing as well as praying, "God, you are so faithful; you have favored me." My passport was stamped to re-enter the United States. However, I was only permitted to stay for three months and had specific instructions to report to the Customs Border and Protection office in Florida for further action.

Days later, my daughter received a call from the Department of Customs Border and Protection to inform her that before reporting to the office, they needed to see evidence that she had resubmitted residency papers on my behalf. We had to begin the process again. The entire process was miraculously completed in three days. Praise the Lord for outcome #4. At the next week's scheduled appointment, we presented the receipt to show that we had paid the required amount. God Favored Me Again!

At my appointment, we met with a considerate, helpful officer who explained that I only had two more months to remain legally in the country. This meant that I needed to receive notice of Residency status before the time expired to prevent deportation. I called some prayer warriors from among my church, friends, and family, who prayed that I would have a favorable outcome.

During this entire process, I listened to a series of teachings entitled The God Factor by Pastor Bill Winston to build my faith in God. The teaching cemented my faith. I also built my confidence by reading the story of Daniel. Daniel chapter 6:23 was my pillow. I rested in these words of Daniel: "because he believed in His God." Those words took center stage in my heart and anchored my trust in God's sovereignty.

I was facing a "Destiny Crossroads," which applied pressure because of the uncertainty and the time stipulations of the United States of America Residency Process, the Green Card process. This was my spiritual den. Unlike me, Daniel, who had faced real lions in a den, prayed, even though he did not know? Ruth similarly had faced a spiritual den of lions called hunger when the barley wheat harvest had ended. Hence, there was no more grain. Ruth was at a "Destiny Crossroads" with hunger because the harvest had ended. The issue of what next was her perplexing situation. In our physical and spiritual dens, we want the

God of heaven to be on our side.

I know that the Lord was working behind the scenes for me, thus causing me to stand in faith. I fulfilled the mission assignment and served the children of Burkina Faso, as many of them came to know the Lord Jesus as their Lord and Personal Savior. Because of my firm conviction, I did not allow fear or anxiety to cripple me. I was convinced that a bright future was ahead, and therefore, wholeheartedly, I trusted God. That was my posture, I expected a favorable outcome regarding the processing of my Green Card.

Equally, Daniel was confident that the lions would not eat him because he was a faithful servant of God. He witnessed an angel of the Lord close the mouths of hungry lions, keeping him safe until he was rescued from the den by the King. On the other hand, Ruth came out of her spiritual den because of her obedience to Naomi's instructions. Her obedience caused her to receive more than enough food in one night. Ruth was redeemed because of her kindness to Boaz. What transpired also changed Naomi's life. The angel closed the lion's mouth on Daniel's behalf, while Naomi was the intermediary between Ruth and Boaz. These scenarios caused me to be confident that God would pull me from my den.

Let us go deeper! My lessons and outcomes in this chapter were life-altering. According to I Corinthians 1:27, "God does the foolish things of this world to confine the wise." I have done many foolish things in my life in the name of Jesus, and I came through, but this one was by far the greatest. Think about what I did! To obey God, I had to defy the Immigration Laws of the United States of America. It took great faith to follow through with that decision. I knew that the penalty for leaving the country could amount to a hefty monetary fine and or deportation. However, my faith in God compelled me to do otherwise.

God is a Spirit. He is eternal and sovereign. He lives outside of time. His word, the Bible, is not bound by planet Earth's natural time clock. The word of God supersedes the instructions of this world system. I love God, and I always seek to obey Him. My belief and trust in Jesus Christ gave me the confidence to know that if I obeyed His instruction, He would take care of me no matter the situation, problem, or circumstance. Nonetheless, not to diminish the significance of what I did, I want you to know that leaving America for missions was not an easy decision to make. I decided to leave the country, fully knowing the potential repercussions involved, but despite this, I chose to obey.

I responded to the voice of my Savior, calling me to the mission field in Burkina Faso to share the message of grace and love. My love for God gave me the boldness to obey and the confidence to believe that He would take care of me and fulfill my heart's desire to reside legally in America once I obeyed Him.

We are spiritual beings who live in a body. Living on earth restricts our bodies to our senses, what we can see, feel, taste, smell, and hear. Therefore, every earthly situation or problem is filtered through our senses. However, our God is sovereign, supernatural, and eternal. He created the world by speaking into existence everything we can touch, hear, see, and smell. God knows what will happen even before He gives His children who have surrendered their lives and have accepted Jesus' instructions. God does not operate in the natural world as we do. Issues or problems do not move Him, but if we hold our ground and keep the faith, He will embrace us with a favorable outcome.

After returning from missions, the odds weighed heavily against me. Nevertheless, I knew that I had heard God's voice and the children of Africa calling me to come and share the message of the Cross with them. Obedience to God helped me maintain a positive position with the expectation of a favorable outcome regarding receiving permanent residency status. God rewards His children, as He told us that to obey is better than sacrifice and to hearken to this world is better than the fat of rams (I Samuel 15:22).

# CHAPTER 9: GOOD NEWS

Not only was my final appointment with Customs and Border Protection drawing near, but so was my expiration date. I eagerly waited, expecting the mailman to deliver my approval letter. Every day I looked forward to receiving this mail. Anxiety taunted me, and its tentacles tried to wrap themselves around my mind, but the Word of God was my constant companion. I used the word as a sword and spoke to myself. During this time, I read and meditated on Romans 4:17-21 daily.

I had prayer warriors who were praying in agreement with me for a favorable response. Whenever the feelings of fear, doubt, unbelief, and anxiety would overwhelm me, I would begin to speak scripture verse aloud to cast those negative thoughts far from me. What I believed in was too large to allow the devil's evil strategies to invade my mind. Every time I repeated a scripture, I envisioned driving the sword of the word into the heart of my enemies. Every time I spoke or read the word aloud, I grew more robust, and the voices around me caused me to grow weaker. I used the word of God and worship music to annihilate the enemy that tried to discourage me.

Christians are in a battle as we are called to fight the good fight of faith, I Timothy 6:12. We have an enemy with many names, all refer to the one devil which was stripped of its power over us by Jesus Christ, our Lord, and Savior when He arose from the dead. Some people call the enemy Lucifer, Beelzebub, Satan, the devil, prince of darkness, lord of the flies, Antichrist, father of lies, serpent, or the dragon. There is an enemy whose job is to defeat us so that we fail to obey Jesus Christ. A battle and a real enemy are waging war against the children of Jesus Christ. Moreover, just in case you were wondering, the believer's fight is in the mind.

Ephesians 6:10-18 - **Finally, be strong in the Lord and his mighty power. 11 Put on the full armor of God so that you can take your stand against the devil's schemes. 12 For our struggle is not against flesh and blood, but against the rulers, against the authorities, against the powers of this dark world and the spiritual forces of evil in the heavenly realms. 13 Therefore put on the full armor of God, so that when the day of evil comes, you may be able to stand your ground,** and after you have done everything, to stand. **¹⁴** Stand firm then, with the belt of truth buckled around your waist, with the breastplate of righteousness in place, **¹⁵** and with your feet fitted with the readiness that comes from the gospel of peace. **¹⁶** In addition to all this, take up the shield of faith, with which you can extinguish all the flaming arrows of the evil one. **¹⁷** Take the helmet of salvation and the sword of the Spirit, which is the word of God. **¹⁸** And pray in the Spirit on all occasions with all kinds of prayers and requests. With this in mind, be alert and always keep on praying for all the Lord's people. **¹⁹** Pray also for me that whenever I speak, words may be given to me so that I will fearlessly make known the mystery of the gospel.

If we do not understand spiritual warfare, we will remain distant and defeated. The believer's fight is not against people. We are in a spiritual fight. We are not fighting with physical people, and we must know that the devil uses people. He possesses people's lives as he comes to life on the inside to carry out his evil deeds through them. We, therefore, must be careful because our spiritual enemy uses physical people to come against us.

We must be skilled in the word of God to discern that our fight is a spiritual war and not make the mistake of fighting against people. In other words, we must discern the spirit that is at work in a person and pray against this spirit and not against the person to experience victory. Therefore, to fix our lives, we have to fix our minds. We must consider what we are thinking. The book of Hebrews in chapter 4:12 says, "For the word of God is alive and active. Sharper than any double-edged sword, it penetrates even to dividing soul and spirit, joints, and marrow; it judges the heart's thoughts and attitudes. Also, 2 Corinthians 10:3-6 explains what our posture should be when we are attacked in our mind.

**³** For though we live in the world, we do not wage war as the world does. **⁴** The weapons we fight with are not the weapons of the world. On the contrary, they have the divine power to demolish strongholds. **⁵** We demolish arguments and every pretension that sets itself up against the knowledge of God, and we take captive every thought to make it obedient to Christ. **⁶** And we will be ready to punish every act of disobedience, once your obedience is complete.

# DESTINY CROSSROADS/TRUSTING THE SOVEREIGNTY OF GOD IN CHALLENGING TIMES

The word of God is our most excellent defense when we feel assaulted or troubled in our minds. The Word of God never fails. It has all of the answers to Life's challenges. The week before I received the announcement about my status, I experienced a mental barrage. The attack was meant to cause me to doubt what I believed. The battle in my head diminished as I loudly declared the Word of God, which did the job. Peace invaded my soul. Colossians 3:15: "Let the peace of Christ rule in your hearts, since as members of one body you were called to peace. And be thankful".

The week before my appointment, the letter of approval arrived in the mail. I rejoiced with thankfulness in my heart. 1 John 5:14-15 says, "This is the confidence we have in approaching God: that if we ask anything according to his will, he hears us. Moreover, if we know that he hears us whatever we ask, we know that we have what we asked of him." When at the appointment, I handed the Customs and Border Patrol officer the letter of approval, and she said, "I am so happy you got approved." I left her office praising and rejoicing because the officer acknowledged my miracle. My faith in God brought victory, and I had the proof.

Ruth's story is a beautifully redemptive love story with a beginning of sadness and hopelessness. Ruth's obedience to follow her mother-in-law led her to a new country in which she had to adopt new traditions and customs. Because she chose to obey Naomi, she survived the testing and uncertainties. Ruth's love for her mother-in-law and her faith resulted in her becoming the great-grandmother of King David. A woman whose intersection was destiny since she was not willing to let the unknown stand in her way, her beginning story laced with sadness and hopelessness, ended in love, joy, peace, and triumph.

Furthermore, she did not allow fear, doubt, or unbelief to deter her. Instead, she stayed the course, married a wealthy husband, and gave birth to a son who changed the course of Jewish history. Ruth, a Moabite priestess, made her way into the Jewish hallmark and is mentioned in the lineage of Jesus our Messiah. What an outcome!

Dear reader, speak the word of God since his words produce positive results. As I write this story, I am settled in Florida, living my best life in simplicity and peace. Each day, I am expecting great things as I continue to live by faith and not sight. My passion for missions is stronger than ever. After I left Africa, I also visited Honduras to share the Good News. In the upcoming year, I will be traveling to a few other countries. It is never too late to pursue your life's passion.

I encourage you to not put limitations on yourself. Hope again, your life has meaning, and your story can inspire someone.

- Someone needs the courage to move on from a failed marriage
- Someone needs to overcome and heal from a traumatic situation
- Someone needs to experience hope after tragedy
- Someone needs the strength to live again after the passing of a loved one
- Someone needs the desire to live and not give up on life
- Someone needs to hear your testimony of healing and restoration
- Someone needs to see your faith as you walk through the challenges of life
- Someone is waiting to celebrate with you, your cheering square is ready
- Someone is watching your resilience; do not give up

Dear Reader,

Giving up is not an option. You were born to win the battles of life. Do not give up on yourself wherever you are in your life right now, be strong and courageous, and know that you were born to win, no matter the odds against you.

## My prayer for you

Heavenly Father, I pray for the reader that his/her heart will fully trust in You, and he/she will not lean to his/her human reasoning and intellect.

I pray that his/her understanding will be illuminated in your presence. Heavenly Father, I pray that in every area, the person praying this prayer. Will acknowledge your sovereignty and yield to your direction.

Heavenly Father, I pray that the reader will trust You in every challenging circumstance because You are working for their good To give his/her an expected end.

I enjoyed sharing my story with you, and I want to leave you with some scripture references to help you begin your new relationship with Jesus.

# WHAT DOES THE BIBLE SAY?

Repeating these positive confessions will change your life.

- I am an ambassador of Christ (I Peter 2: 9-10 & 2 Corinthian 5:20)

- I am a citizen of heaven (Philippians 3:20-21 & Ephesians 2:6)

- I am the righteousness of God in Christ (2 Corinthians 5:21)

- I am strong (Philippians 4:3 & Ephesians 6:10)

- I am loved (Ephesians 1:4 & Ephesians 2:4)

- I am understood by God (Psalm 139:1)

- I am alive & saved (Ephesians 2:4-5)

- I am chosen by God (John 15:16)

- I am a child of God (Galatians 3:26)

- I am saved (John 3:16)

- I am redeemed (Galatians 3:13)

- I am possible (Matt 19:25-26)

- I am blessed (Ephesians 1:3

- I am precious (Isaiah 43:4)

- I am an heir of God (Romans 8:17)

- I am beautiful ((Psalm 139:14)

- I am created in His Image (Genesis 1:27)

- I am a friend of Christ (John 15:15)

- I am a conqueror (Romans 8:37)

- I am triumphant (2 Corinthians 2:14)

# ABOUT THE AUTHOR

**Gaylean Maynard** (born Gaylean Sharon Brown-Maynard) is a Bahamian author, speaker, and religious figure known for her books that focus on her spiritual journey and her message of triumph through faith. She is described as a woman of faith with a passion for people and a desire to advance the Kingdom of God. She has also been interviewed on television programs, where she has shared her experiences in the religious sphere, particularly in her role as an Apostle.

**Authorship:** Maynard wrote the autobiographical book *Behind the Smiles*, which details her life and her message of God bringing triumph through tragedy. She also co-authored *Destiny Crossroads: Trusting the Sovereignty of God in Challenging Times*.

**Religious Leadership:** She is recognized as an Apostle within certain religious circles, as noted in a discussion on the *Women Empowering Women* lifestyle talk show.

**Message and Focus:** Her work and public presence are centered on her faith, her servant's heart, and her message of hope, encouraging people to see God in the midst of difficult circumstances.

**International Reach:** Maynard's desire is to travel the world and touch lives, reflecting a global perspective on her spiritual mission.

## ABOUT THE BOOK

Have you ever stopped to consider the sovereignty of God? Isaiah 40:15 "Behold, the nations are like a drop from a bucket, and are regarded as a speck of dust on the scales; Behold, He lifts the islands like fine dust" This verse gives the reader a glimpse into the incredible power and might of God who is seated far above all principalities and powers. In this verse, God reminds His people that He is sovereign and that no one can be compared to Him.

Destiny Crossroad takes readers on a journey. Each chapter quietly unveils the Sovereignty of God in Gaylean Maynard's life As she unfolds her life experiences. She aims to leave her readers with this resounding question, "Who is like the sovereign God who defies impossible situations, pain, roadblocks, space, and uncertain times"?

Maynard uses her personal life story to inspire her readers through prayers and quiet reflections to cultivate their relationship with God, their Heavenly Father. Just as Ruth's decision to leave Moab to follow an unknown path changed her path and destiny, I hope that reading this book will intrigue, provoke, and encourage you reader to encounter and embrace the sovereign God of the Universe. There is absolutely no time like the present to experience the King of kings and Lord of lords!